The Distance Across One's Heart:
Poetry For the Writer

a collection of poems by Sigmund A. Boloz

illustrated by Abraham Jones

Karen Snow, editor

© 1997 Sigmund A. Boloz (text)

© 1997 Abraham Jones (art)

ISBN - 1 - 886635 - 12 - 9

cover illustration of Antoinette C. Boloz, age 9

Dedicated to Victoria Boloz because. . .

IT WAS MY MOTHER'S IDEA

It was my mother's idea to come to America.
It was my mother's idea to come.
She is not exactly sure where the idea entered her mind
But supposes that she read about America somewhere in school,
Somewhere in her Polish childhood.
My father did not want to come.
My father did not want to come
To another strange country.

Neither of my parents spoke English at the time.
Both had been soldiers in the Polish army.
They had three young children and one on the way.
They had survived War World II.
They had survived the concentration camps.

My mother tells the stories
Of the early morning raid upon her village,
Of the awful train rides to the camps,
Of the horrible hunger.

My mother tells the stories
Of the Russian woman who she wishes she could find,
To thank her,
To thank her for that half of one boiled potato.
My mother is sure that boiled potato
Saved her from starvation,
From that awful hunger.

My mother tells the stories of the American soldiers
And of how she ran to see them as they arrived.
She had pictured them as larger than life
And was disillusioned to see the men,
"Who looked just like us!"

My mother tells the stories
Of the trip to safety,
Of the single blanket she wore for days for lack of clothes,
Of the shame and humiliation of being sprayed for lice,
Of having her hair cut off,
And of those who named her, "Crocodile,"
Because of her bony appearance.

After the war,
It was my mother's idea to come to America.
My father did not want to come
To another strange country.
They had seen too many countries.
My father did not want to come.

My mother tells the stories
Of the long boat ride to America,
Of the sea sickness,
And most importantly of the single silver spoon
Which my father smuggled onto the ship to feed the baby.

My mother tells the stories
Of arriving at the wrong port,
Of the people who almost did not accept her son,
And of covering her children in jackets
Because she refused to cover her children in discarded, bloodied sheets.

It was my mother's idea to come to America.
My father did not want to come.

But my mother tells the stories
Of America with love and with pride,
Of what she calls, "The greatest country of all!"

It was my mother's idea to come to America.
My father did not want to come.

Writers are not born with a pen in their hand or a specific language of speech. Most have had to practice the "D's" of growth and change: Dedication. Devotion. Discipline. . . but also, Desire. Destination. Daring to be Different. Discovering the Delight in your Craft. and Digging in the Dirt. This is a book about the joy and messiness of being a writer. The poems included in this volume speak about writing, being a writer, a writer as reader, the impact of writing on a reader and the challenges that readers and writers face. I hope they will inspire you to write many, many of your own.

Sigmund A. Boloz,
Ganado, Arizona, January 1997

Table of Contents

SELDOM MISTAKES

Opening lines
Are seldom a mistake,
They are precisely chosen for
The images they awake.

In number and texture
They invariably delight,
As if fused together
They naturally do unite.

Sigmund A. Boloz

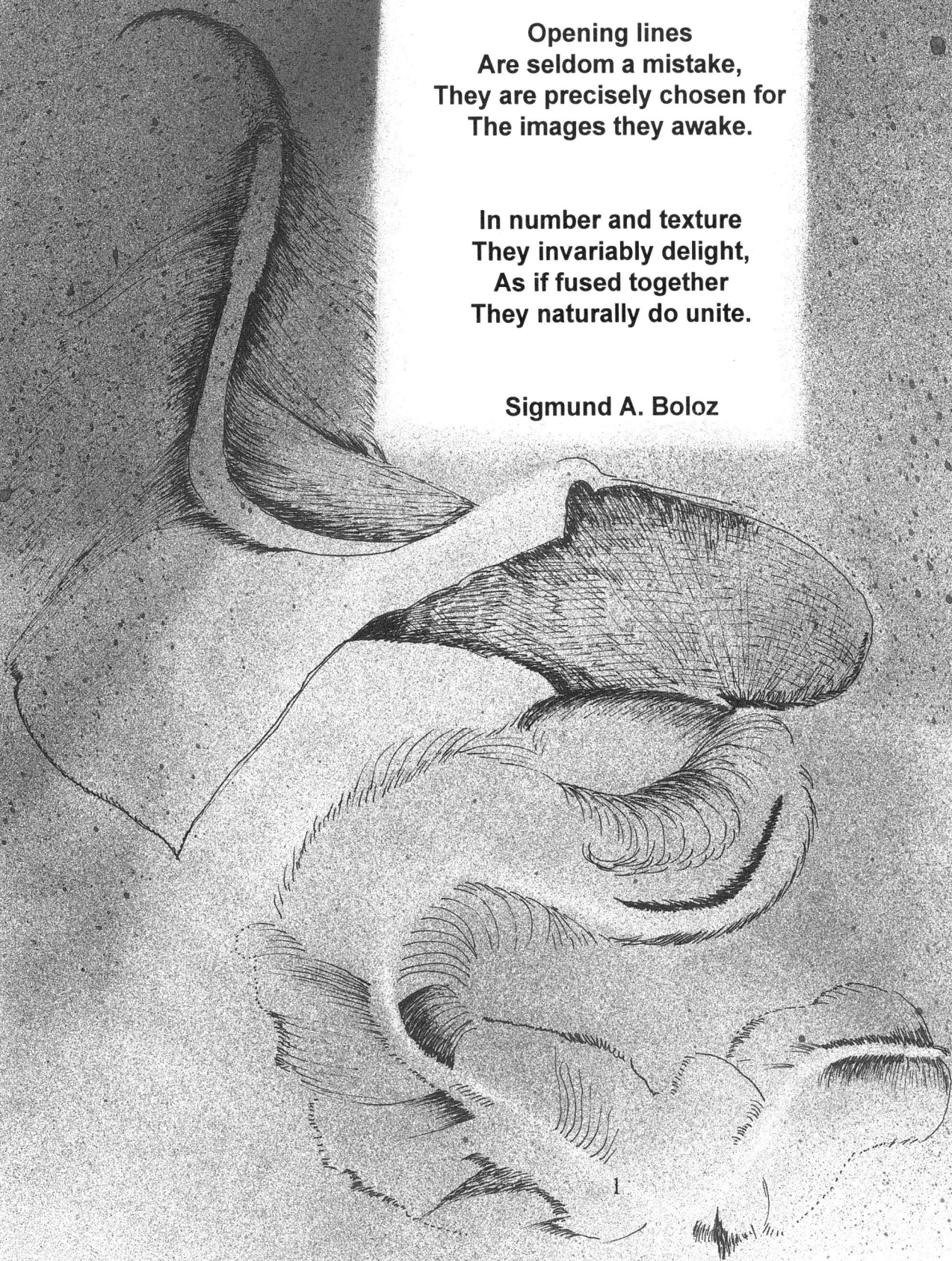

1

ESSENCE OF LANGUAGE

Language
is connected
to a series
of thoughts,
not to simple strings
of letters
to be gathered
and taught.

The essence
of language
lives in the concepts
that thrive
in the substance
of your reflections
and in the notions
that others derive.

Sigmund A. Boloz

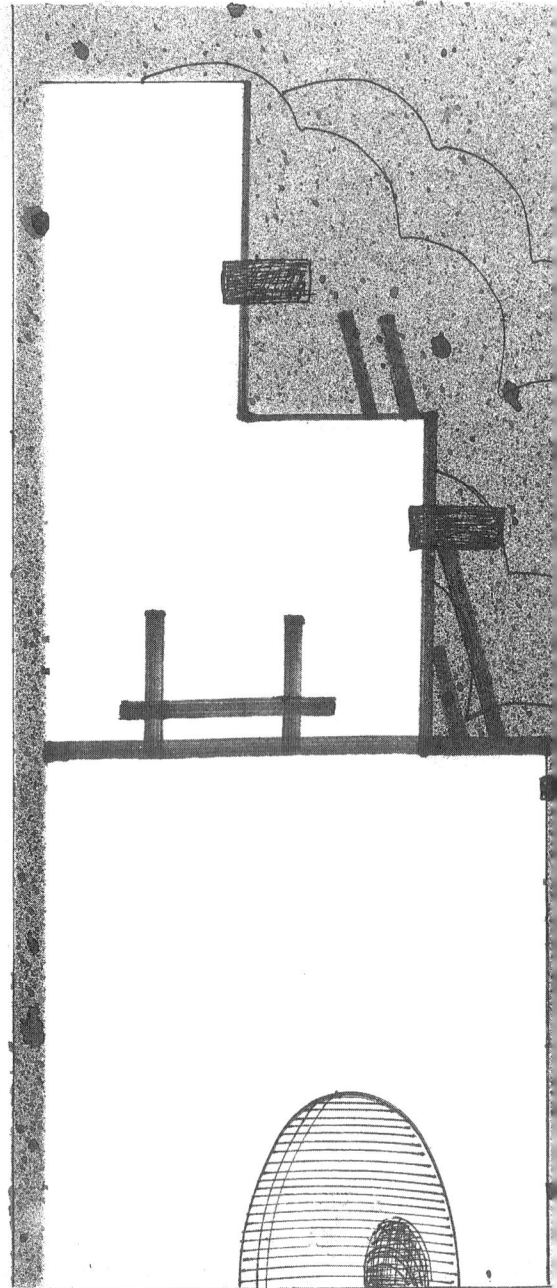

NEVER THOSE WORDS ALONE

Poems are always bigger
Than the meager space they occupy,
For they are consistently, invariably
More than what reaches the reader's eye.

Poems are rarely, ever,
Those insufficient words alone,
For they have a pulsating heart, a center,
A definite life of their own.

Sigmund A. Boloz

WRITE YOUR LIFE IN PENCIL

Stand in the stillness.
Close your eyes.
Listen to your heartbeat.
Realize

That you, too, are important.
Unlock your mind.
Attend to the wanderings.
Seek. You will find

Anecdotes,
So many nuggets made of gold,
Precious vignettes,
Discoveries which must be told.

Then speak from your heart.
Mistakes, they will be made.
So, write your life in pencil
And let the words cascade.

Just stand in the stillness.
Close your eyes.
Listen to your heartbeat.
Realize

That your stories, too, are important,
As is the reader's view.
Write your life in pencil
For this you write for you.

Sigmund A. Boloz

THE MEASURE OF WORDS

The words flow through my intellect,
Attaching themselves as they pass,
Inexorably attracting those recollections
As if through a mirrored glass.

Intensifying my emotions,
A frenzied pitch,
Causing my knees to buckle
As with a switch,
Inducing my heart to throb
At a startling rate,
As tears overcome my eyes,
My exhilarating fate,

Then propelled in the sensation,
The message swarms my mind,
Striking over and again at the heart
Of emotions once confined.

Inexorably drawing those recollections,
As if through the looking glass.
As a writer's words flow through my intellect,
Found memories as they pass.

Sigmund A. Boloz

THE DISTANCE IS ESSENTIAL

You can withdraw and leave it,
Let it rest with others or alone,
Then you can pounce on another
Which you wish to compose or hone.

For distance is usually essential,
While speed, often, not at all,
Especially when you seek to discover
Those sly words which do not fall.

And pieces do seem to swirl together,
Have no spirit of their own,
If they are rushed into existence
As some under-polished stone.

So, I appreciate the detachment,
The liberty to meander and roam,
To search for the right words
Which create the extraordinary poem.

The occasion to withdraw and leave one idea,
Let it rest with others or alone,
The anticipation to pounce on another
Which I wish to compose or hone.

For distance is usually essential,
While speed, often, not at all,
Especially when you seek to discover
The sly words which do not fall.

Sigmund A. Boloz

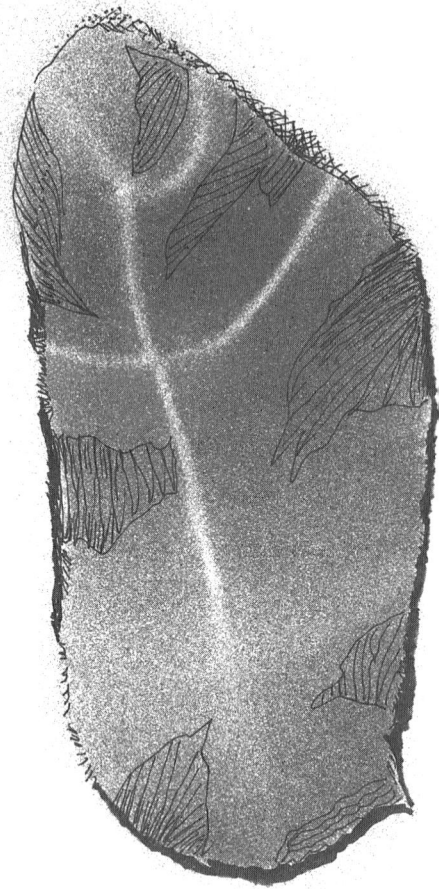

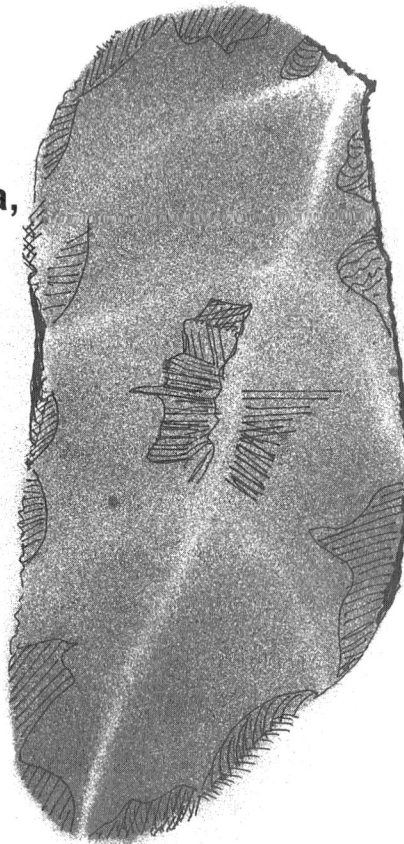

6

YOUR WRITER'S BLOOD

You must be possessed by the idea.
You must see it as yours alone.
The idea must delight and excite you.
It must be one which you own.

You must carry the investment.
It must be invested in you.
Above all, it must be an idea
Which is worthy of carrying through.

The idea must not belong to another,
Although it may be an idea which you share,
The idea must be a part of your vision,
An idea about which you truly do care.

But, above all else, it must be an idea which drives you,
Releases that emotional flood,
For only then will the idea carry the charge
To electrify your writer's blood.

Sigmund A. Boloz

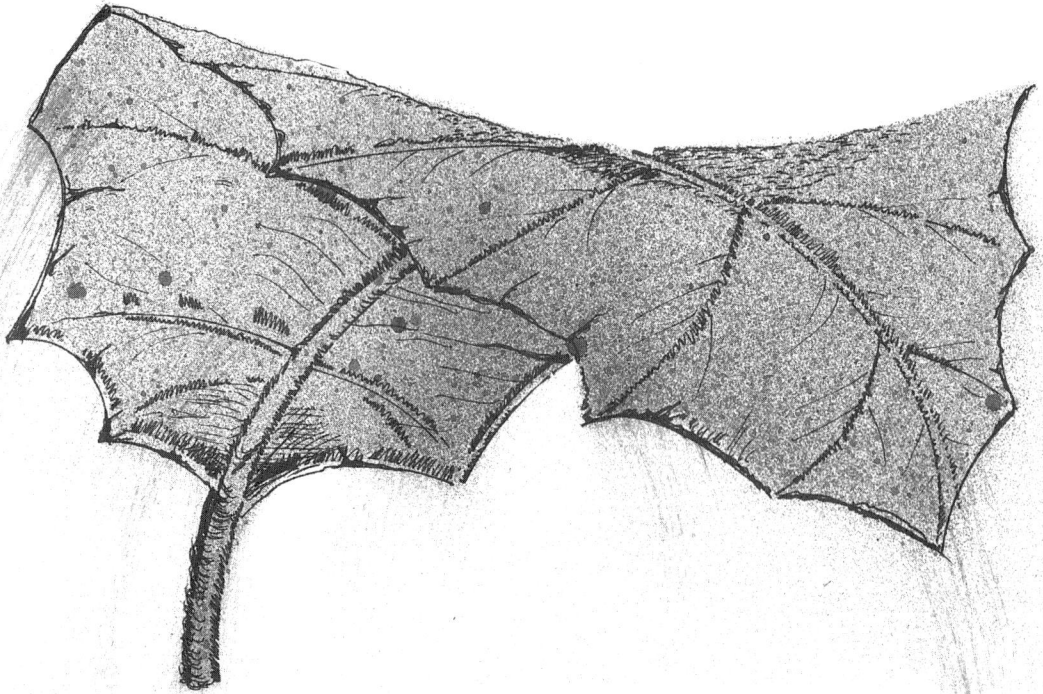

THE HAUNTING

I once had an idea
Which floated loosely in my head,
But I did not write it down
Before I went to bed.

And now it forever haunts me
As a lost phantom I cannot find,
Floating mysteriously
In the silhouettes of my mind.

But I still know it's there
Even though I can no longer pull it out,
For I endure its garbled echo
That continues to reverberate about.

Sigmund A. Boloz

WHERE?

It has eluded you.
So, you have returned to your desk
Looking mediative, thoughtful,
Absorbed and rather statuesque.

Where could it be hidden?
You contemplate. You frown.
You have searched for hours,
Turned your room upside-down.

But you know that it is somewhere.
You know that it is near,
And, perhaps, if only you would look less hard,
Its presence might become more clear.

You have searched your personal closets.
You have flipped through several books.
You have sat staring out that one particular window.
You have gazed those far-off looks.

And still it has eluded you.
So, you have returned to your desk,
Looking reflective, contemplative,
Pensive and rather statuesque.

And then you collide with it,
In a lighting bolt of delight
As the thrill of an idea strikes you
And then you write, and write, and write.

Sigmund A. Boloz

ILLUSIONS OF NIGHT

I love the wind at my back
As I settle myself to write,
And the harmony that trickles
Into the solitude of night.

I love the time born of patience,
The tranquility of active thought,
And the challenge of conflict,
When a powerful notion is caught.

And I love to contemplate the possibilities
In a calm, star-filled sky,
While the flicker of a kerosene light falls
Upon this dreamer's eye.

Sigmund A. Boloz

AS A WRITER

As a writer,
You must develop the good eye
And cultivate a good ear,

You must discipline yourself
Not only to see,
But also to envision,
Not only to hear,
But to listen.

Learn to recognize those gems
As they dangle near your ear.

As a writer,
You must enlarge the good heart
And germinate the open mind,

You must permit yourself
Not only to feel,
But also to be vulnerable,
Not only to consider the obvious,
But to find,

To expose those jewels
As they lay suspended within your mind.

Sigmund A. Boloz

PEOPLE WILL THINK YOU'RE NUTS!

People are going to think you're nuts
Because you prowl at night,
As you go about your interest
With a fiendish delight,

Organizing your favorite weapons
Just as a maniac might,
People are going to think you're nuts
As they see your eyes ignite,

As you pull up a piece of paper
To some dimly-lit light,
People are going to think you're nuts
Because you love to write.

Sigmund A. Boloz

WHEN AN IDEA HAS YOU

Your mind is running
At an incredible pace.
I can read it upon your eyes,
It is written in your face.

An idea has you,
But it will let go,
And you will have nothing,
Nothing left to show,

Except for the stories
Of the one which got away,
Of the magnificent one you had
On some other distant day.

So, train yourself to be ready
For the ideas that catch you,
For the great ones don't appear often
But we each do get a few.

So, when your mind begins sprinting
At some extraordinary pace,
When you read it upon your eyes
Or feel it written in your face,

Seize the opportunity,
Wrestle it to the ground,
Then draw out your pen
And scribble the thoughts down.

Sigmund A. Boloz

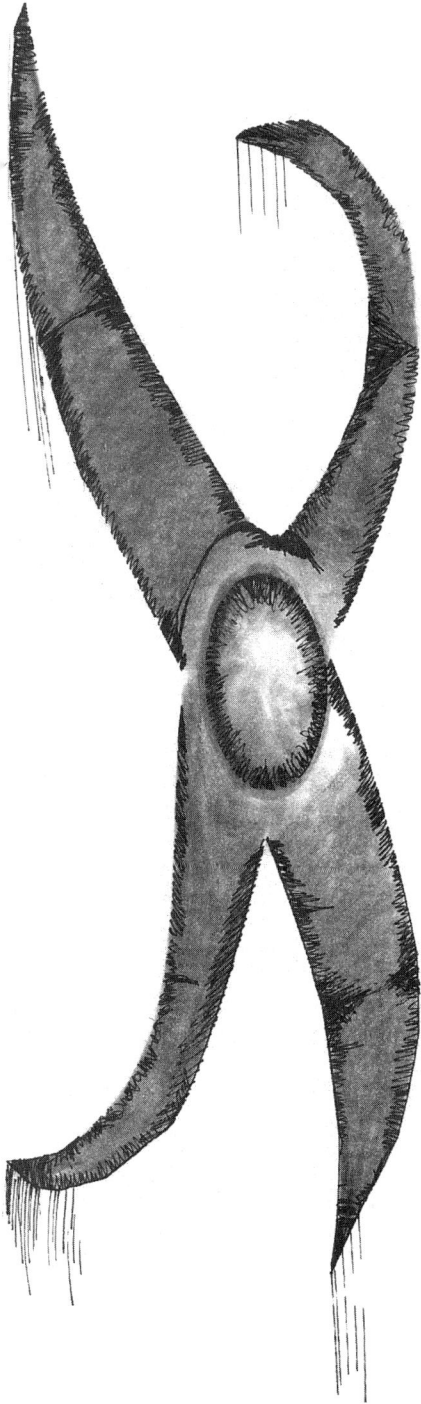

UNCREATIVE

Feeling disaffected,
Rather uncreative today,
Void of ideas
Without much to say.

Searching the swirling clouds
For something interesting,
But not a thought.
I can't think of a thing.

Just browsing the circumstances,
Hopeless for a thought,
Fishing for a connection
Wishing to be caught.

Trying to remain focused,
Yet, my mind tends to stray.
Feeling disaffected,
Uncreative today.

Sigmund A. Boloz

THE WRITER AND THE PEN

There was an attentive look
As she gazed in puzzlement at me,
With a pen dangling from her mouth
In a light air of tranquility.

"Another writer!" I beamed,
As she pulled the pen to her hand,
While questioning my statement
With a tight, glaring reprimand.

"Excuse me!" I laughed,
As I looked into her blue eyes,
"But pens aren't really made for chewing,
As your constant chewing implies."

"Becoming a real writer
Begins, my tiny friend,
With using and with chewing. . .
Pens at the correct end."

Sigmund A. Boloz

THE MAGICIANS

From the dawn of human history
As if some gift was possessed,
They have held the potency,
Had the power to suggest.

Each practiced in their art,
Actions carefully planned,
Especially skillful hand movements,
Misdirection on demand.

Specializing in the impossible,
Creating illusions of a sort,
Transforming simple words
Into extraordinary import.

Causing images to float,
Making them disappear,
And through sleight-of-hand
Having them reappear.

Capturing perfect moments,
Through mental alertness and skillful hands,
Joining the disconnected,
Fascination an audience understands.

So it is with practiced writers
And the simple words they transform,
Making the unimaginable seem possible.
How incredibly they perform.

Sigmund A. Boloz

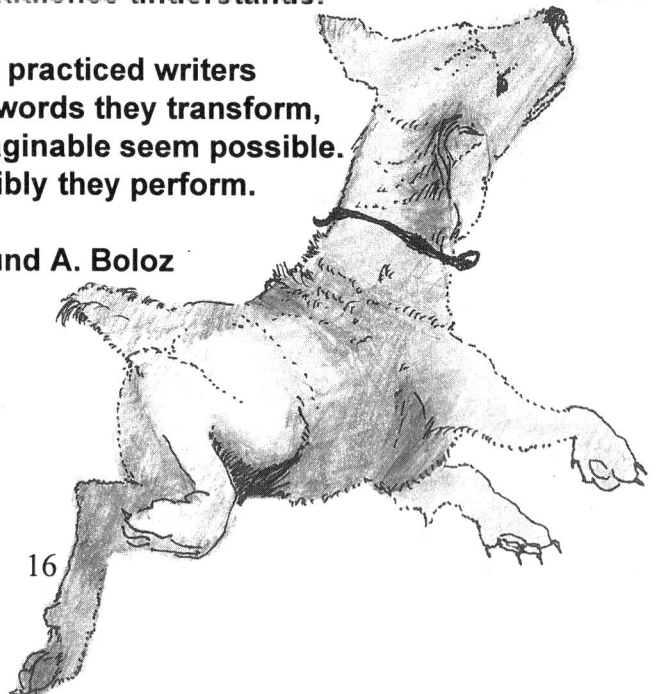

16

YOUNG AUTHORS

I was thinking about how you all came to be here,
about what you all had done,
of how you had accepted some responsibility,
about how you, above anyone else, had won,
had prevailed, I mean, over the internal battles
that all writers face,
and how you had confronted the self-discipline of writing
that all writers chase.

I was thinking about how you all shared so many things in common:
the pencil and the pen,
the scraps of paper, the notebook,
the excitement when
you journey
across blank pages,
traveling and adventuring
through writing stages.

I was thinking of the exhilaration of when that idea first strikes you,
and of when you write it down,
making it permanent
on almost anything around,
a half-used napkin,
a piece of misplaced wood,
or even an old candy wrapper
Is sometimes good.

But the important idea is
that you captured notions,
that you all wrote them down
and wrapped them in your emotions,
while, all the time mixing and matching
story elements and the written word
with the life stories
that you've lived, read, or heard,
and you built them up and up
as all writers do,
and shared your discoveries with the outside world
and with other writers like you.

So I was thinking about how you all came to be here,
about that one reason I might cite,
and you know that you are all here today,
marked forever as authors, because you write.

Sigmund A. Boloz

HOW DO YOU KNOW?

Where do the ideas come from?
How do they flow?
Where do the words go?
How do you know?

Just what goes on
In your young poet head?
What keeps you awake,
Stirs you from your bed?

It all seems so easy
As I watch you smile
And add another poem to an
Overflowing pile.

It all seems so easy,
Until I look into your eyes,
Sense your seriousness
Then I actually realize

That I will never know what goes on
In your young poet head,
But it too often keeps you awake
Stirs you from your bed.

So, where do the ideas come from?
How do you know where certain words will go?
Why do I ask?
For sometimes even you would like to know.

Sigmund A. Boloz

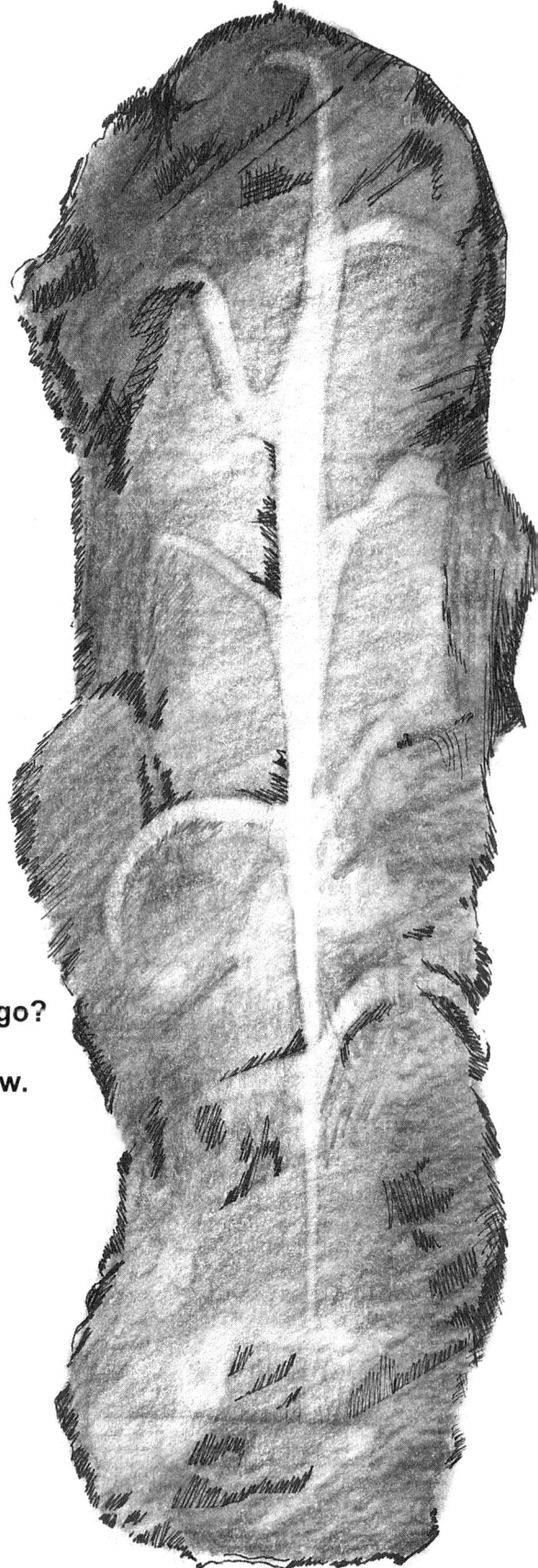

18

POETIC THIRST

There are times that I am wonderfully envious
After having read some remarkable piece,
A creation whose beauty totally imprisons me
While leaving no hope of early release.

I tremble at the addiction
Of this sumptuous thing
And my heart aches for another opportunity
To hear its phrases sing,

A creation so exquisite
In its concept and rhyme,
That in all honesty, I wish
That this work had been mine.

A masterpiece that I long to have authored,
To have appreciated first,
A piece that fills me with jealous admiration
And my throat with poetic thirst.

Sigmund A. Boloz

WHAT CAME FIRST?

There is no writing
without reading.
There is no reading
without writing.

What came first
the chicken or the eggs which we are fed?
What came first
the words on paper or the words which are read?

The power of reading,
As well as the writers' lives, you see,
Renew one to the other's life blood
Through a power called literacy.

For there is no need for writing
That fails to respect a reader's dignity,
And the beauty of the words on paper
Lies in their reciprocity.

So, what came first
the chicken or the eggs which we are fed?
What came first
the words on paper or the words which are read?

Sigmund A. Boloz

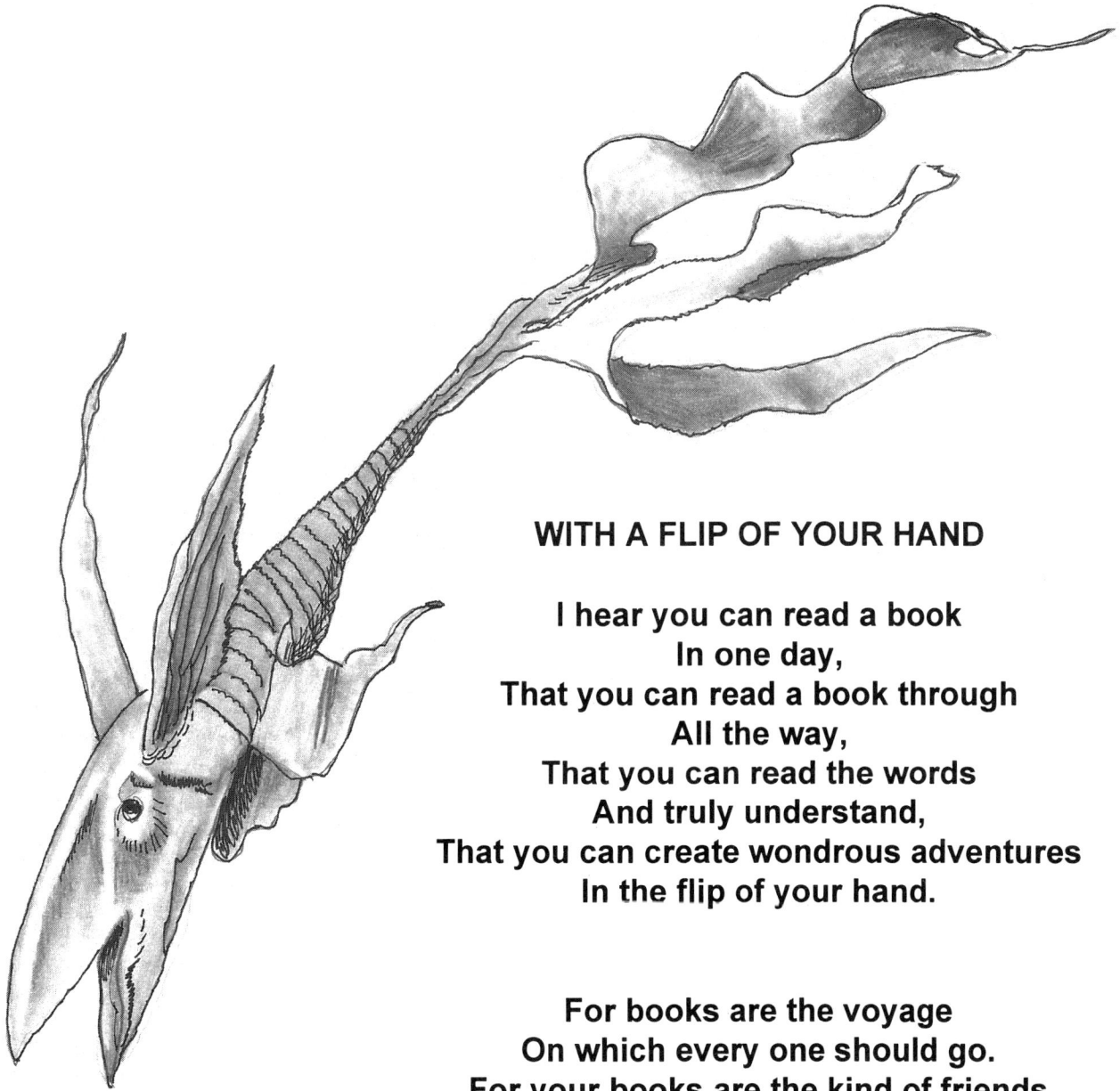

WITH A FLIP OF YOUR HAND

I hear you can read a book
In one day,
That you can read a book through
All the way,
That you can read the words
And truly understand,
That you can create wondrous adventures
In the flip of your hand.

For books are the voyage
On which every one should go.
For your books are the kind of friends
All people should want to know.
For books reveal worlds,
Put them at your command,
And their magic begins quite simply,
With a flip of your hand.

Sigmund A. Boloz

RENEWAL

I renew my life within every book
That I happen to be passing through,
For I find that I share each character's life
And that I am also venturing, too.

Books become my experience,
Once chosen from the shelf,
For when I breathe the character's breath I am
Never again myself.

Sigmund A. Boloz

WITHIN THE LINES

The game is played
Within the lines,
Or so some
Would have you believe,
And no one is to play
In the out-of-bounds,
Is the message
We all receive.

For lines are made
To control the game
As are whistles
and flags and such,
And the rules
are posted to control the same
And to determine
who and what to touch.

But beware of the men
In the zebra suits
Who carry whistles
and flags and books
For they don't always call it
As they see it
Or even how it looks.

For the game is not always played
Within the lines
As some
Would have you believe,
For I have learned to play
In the out-of-bounds
And to keep an ace tucked
Within my sleeve.

Sigmund A. Boloz

FREEDOM

Sometimes you must venture into the darkness
Before you can see the light,
And you can only appreciate one thing's importance
When it is taken from your sight,

For sometimes it is that which is most obvious,
That one thing which is most often free,
Which we take most for granted,
And makes it hardest for us to see.

Sigmund A. Boloz

24

YOUR INFLUENCE NEVER STOPS

Everything is interconnected,
Every single thing that we do,
Nothing stops with just one person,
It keeps on moving through

From the moment of its beginning,
It continues to go beyond,
Looping in every direction
Like the ripples of a pond,

Reaching out to touch others,
To reverberate about,
And like the strongest of echoes
Only slowly fading out

After beginning other connections,
Touching many others as well,
And where its influence will stop
No one ever can truly tell.

So, imagine the consequences
Of every single thing that you start,
For those things will eventually circle back
And make you a continued part.

Sigmund A. Boloz

COME TOO LATE

Few things come
To those who wait,
And, often, the things that do,
Do come too late,

For the things that are needed,
Are more often needed now
And simply waiting
Doesn't adequately allow

For those precise things
To be in that time or place,
To provide the correct answers
For the questions you might face.

So, dream, hope and envision
But work and create,
Otherwise, those things you need
May find you too late.

Sigmund A. Boloz

LIVE TODAY

As you consider the future,
Remember yesterday,
But in envisioning tomorrow
Live completely today,

For today is for certain,
Tomorrow a desire,
Live fully in the present
Not for what you admire,

But live like you mean it,
Live unabridged every day,
As you consider the future
And remember yesterday.

Sigmund A. Boloz

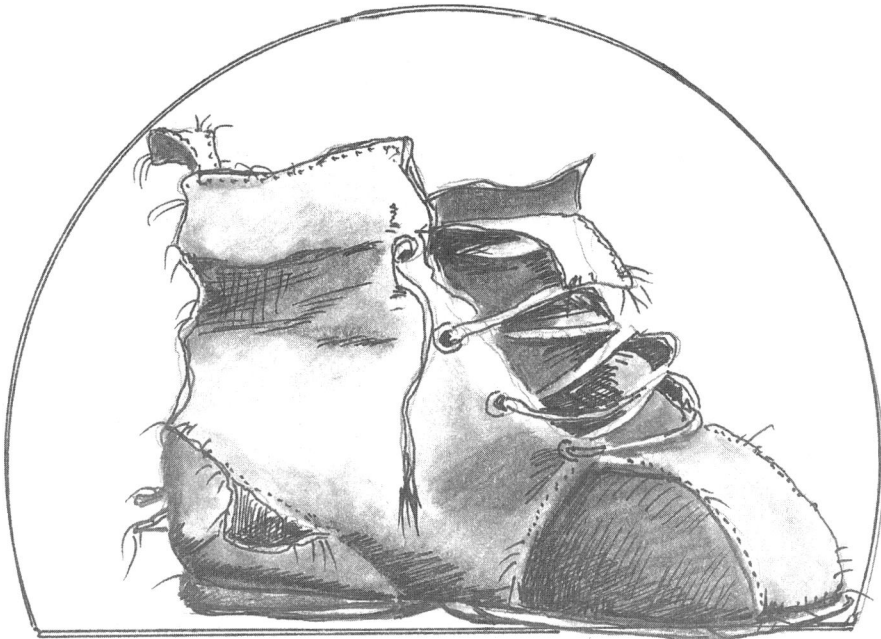

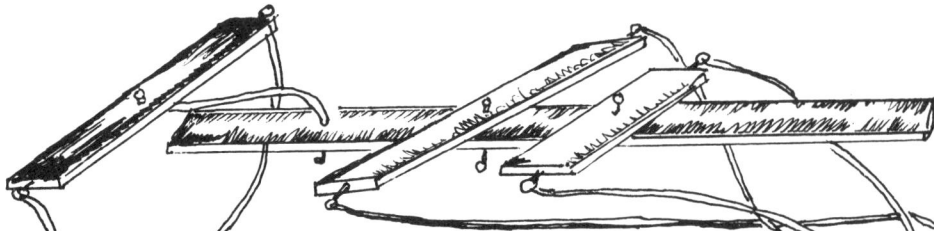

CHOICES SOMETIMES CHOOSE YOU

Sometimes you must venture out into the darkness
To find the elusive light.
Sometimes you must step into the unknown
In order to improve your sight.

Sometimes you must follow your strongest instincts,
Call it blind faith if you must.
Sometimes you must travel toward the unknown horizon
Or to at least empower others with your trust.

Sometimes you must just start climbing
To discover what can be found.
Sometimes you must just make your way
As you fumble around.

Sometimes you must jump in with both feet,
Allowing for opportunities along the way.
Sometimes you must simply seize the moment
Whatever might come your way.

And sometimes the only way of knowing
Is to wade into an unknown place
And grasp onto the best alternative
Before it slaps you in your face.

Yes, sometimes you must venture out into the darkness
To find the elusive light.
Sometimes you must step into the unknown
In order to improve your sight.

Sigmund A. Boloz

28

WE LIVE OUR STORIES

We live our lives
According to our stories,
The stories we have made,
The stories we have set out
The stories that we trade.

We live our lives
In a sort of invention,
The half-truths of the mind,
The legends that have sprung up
And in the heros who we find.

We live our lives
In mottos and slogans,
In the symbols of desire,
As we strive and struggle
As we climb ever higher.

And we need these stories,
Splendid, glorious stories,
These rich stories that we live,
For we need our stories
For the courage that they give.

Sigmund A. Boloz

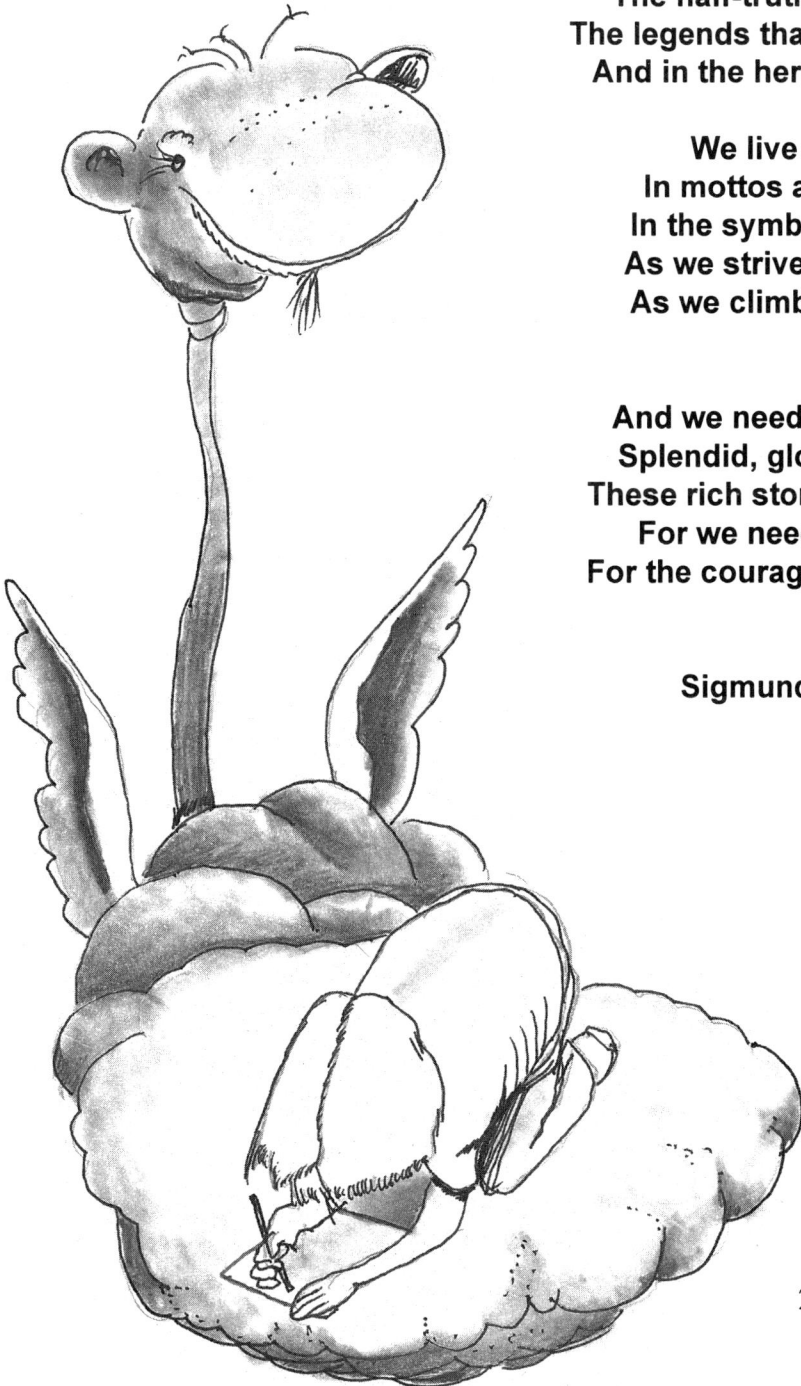

THE DISTANCE

The distance between success and failure
Is the distance across one's heart . . .

It is the distance between convincing yourself
That you are stupid
And allowing for the possibility
That your are smart.

The distance between success and failure
Is the distance across one's hand . . .

It is the distance between being loved
unconditionally
For who you are
And being punished for what you are not
Or do not understand.

The distance between success and failure
Is thc distance across one's dream . . .

It is the distance between speculating about
Your level of capability
Or never doubting that you are capable,
Something called self-esteem.

Sigmund A. Boloz

Other books by Sigmund A. Boloz:

Who Speaks For The Children?
illustrated by Christine F. Hackett
Published by the Arizona Reading Association (1993)

A Wondrous Ride: and other Poems for Children
illustrated by Abraham Jones
Published by Wooded Hill Productions (1994)

Clouds Before The Storm
illustrated by Abraham Jones
Published by Wooded Hill Productions (1994)

Prairie Dog Dreams
illustrated by Abraham Jones
Published by Wooded Hill Productions (1995)

Odious Mud
illustrated by Preston A. Boloz
Published by Wooded Hill Productions (1995)

From Daybooks to Night Logs: Journeying with Journals
Published by Wooded Hill Productions (1996)

The Learning Never Stops
illustrated by Abraham Jones
Published by Wooded Hill Productions (1996)

Posters by Sigmund A. Boloz

Learning (color)

There is a Need... (black and white)

This is my Right (color)

It Begins in the Hogan (color)

I Loved My Way Into Language (color)

Published by WOODED HILL PRODUCTIONS
Post Office Box 825
Ganado, Arizona 86505
(520) 755-3774

Sigmund A. Boloz has been publishing his writing for 25 years. He began writing poetry in 1984 and has published over 200 poems in more than 50 magazines, books and anthologies across the country.

Sig is the author of eight books and his personal goal is to complete 20 poems each month. That's finishing 240 poems a year!

Writers also read and he tries to read a chapter or an article every day. He also loves to read trade books and the comics.

He is on the editorial advisory board of *The Reading Teacher* and is a member of the **Author's** Guild.

Abraham Jones has illustrated five books.   He found this book to be another good chance to share his beautiful artwork. He loves to play with ideas and his current interests are carving and painting with acrylics.

Abe grew up in Ganado where he still lives. He teaches conversational Navajo to the students at Ganado Primary School.

Karen Snow. She lives.

Special thanks to Susan Stropko and Terrell Piechowski for their interest in this volume.